THE DECOUPAGE SOURCEBOOK

For two great chicks.
Thanks for everything
Lynn Korver

THE DECOUPAGE SOURCEBOOK

Jocasta Innes & Stewart Walton

Photography by Richard Foster

CONRAN OCTOPUS

First published in 1995 by
Conran Octopus Limited,
37 Shelton Street,
London WC2H 9HN

Designer *Alison Barclay*
Project Editor *Tessa Clayton*
Commissioning Editor *Louise Simpson*
Picture Researcher *Rachel Davies*
Production Controller *Mano Mylvaganam*
Photographic Direction *Sue Storey*
Stylist *Camilla Bambrough*
Project Assistant *Ron Barber*
Carpentry *Tim Hickmott*

A catalogue record for this book is available
from the British Library

ISBN 1 85029 731 2

Typeset by Textype Typesetters, Cambridge
Produced by Mandarin Offset Ltd
Printed and bound in China

PUBLISHER'S ACKNOWLEDGEMENTS

The publisher would like to thank the following for providing
props for photography:
Designers Guild, 271 and 277 Kings Road, London SW3 5EN
Themes and Variations, 231 Westbourne Grove W11 2SE
Thomas Goode, 19 South Audley Street, London W1Y 6BN
C.X.V., Kings Road, London SW3
Divertimenti, 139 and 141 Fulham Road, London SW3 6SD
The Dining Room Shop, 62 White Hart Lane, London SW13
David Harvey, 5 Old Bond Street, London W1
Basia Zarzycka, 135 Kings Road, London SW3
Peter Place, 636 Kings Road, London SW6

PICTURE CREDITS

The publisher would like to thank the following photographers
and organizations for their kind permission to reproduce the
images in this book:
British Architectural Library, RIBA, London; British Museum;
Edimedia; Mary Evans Picture Library; The Hulton Deutsch
Collection; The Illustrated London News Picture Library; The
Robert Opie Collection; Range/Bettman; St. Bride Printing
Library.

The authors and publisher have made every effort to ensure that
all instructions contained within this book are accurate and safe,
and cannot accept liability for any resulting injury, damage or loss
to persons or property however it may arise.

Although photocopying is suggested as a means of reproducing
images, the authors and publisher advise readers to take careful
note of the photocopying and copyright reproduction laws.

CONTENTS

INTRODUCTION

Take a printed image, hand-colour or not to taste, cut out neatly, paste down on anything from trinket box to armoire, and you have worked a transformation. The beauty of decoupage (the word derives from the French verb *découper*: to cut out) is that it allows even the least artistically gifted to preen in borrowed plumage. Given deftness, patience and modest colouring skills, plus lots of varnish, anyone can make an ordinary object more interesting and attractive.

Once known as 'the poor man's art', decoupage by the eighteenth century had become a respected and often highly skilled art form, as evident in Mary Delany's intricate flower collages (above and right).

Decoupage first began to flourish in the late fifteenth century, when bold and elaborate printed decorative borders were produced in Germany for use on furniture, simulating the complex wood inlay, or 'tarsia' work, that was fashionable during the Renaissance. Glued down and heavily varnished, this printed short cut was almost indistinguishable from the real thing, at least at a distance. Probably the subterfuge was reflected in the price. Certainly when the Venetians later began using tinted cut-outs of chinoiserie figures, swags and blossoms to enliven painted furniture in a lively approximation of much-prized Oriental lacquer wares, the process was explicitly seen as cut-price and none the worse for that. Indeed, this light-hearted rip-off of the laborious effects of genuine Eastern lacquer was christened *arte povera* – the poor man's art. Ironically, surviving examples today change hands at astronomical prices!

During the eighteenth century, decoupage joined such activities as bead work, straw work, watercolour painting and making music, as suitable time-fillers and accomplishments for European gentle-women. It is too easy to dismiss and patronize these 'ladies' amusements', as they came to be known. Trained by expensive tutors, many of these women had real talent, and some truly excellent work resulted from this welter of creativity. One collection, now housed in the British Museum, is the work of Mary Delany (1700–1788), whose charm as a friend and hostess endeared her to such folk as Jonathan Swift, and ultimately the British Royal Family. Mrs Delany was well versed in all the fashionable crazes of her day, but being less rich than her aristocratic friends, she delved deeper and more seriously into such genteel occupations as 'cut-paper work'. Her 'botanical portraits' of exotic and native flora, produced entirely from cut and tinted paper, are both wonderfully exact and meticulously executed. They also rank among the most captivating examples of botanical art extant.

Meanwhile, the craze for decoupage had also infiltrated the French court of Louis XVI. Marie Antoinette and her court ladies insouciantly snipped up the work of court painters of the calibre of Watteau, Boucher and Fragonard, in their enthusiasm for decorating fans, boxes and screens. The mystery is that none of this royal decoupage seems to have survived the Revolution. Conceivably, among the offerings on a flea-market stall someone will one day discover a battered trinket box decoupaged by a royal hand.

Victorian 'scrap sheets' – mass-produced collections of colourful images – were a mid-nineteenth-century innovation that nudged decoupage into a new, wholesomely domestic phase. Making scrap screens became a popular rainy-day occupation for the nursery, allowing mamma or nanny a few hours' peace while the children snipped and pasted, messily content. Scrap work varies in artistry and execution, as one would expect. Some examples are boldly conceived, handsome and colourful, but many are a jolly jumble: animals, flowers and sentimental scenes, mingled higgledy-piggledy with no apparent motive other than to cover every available inch.

After its Victorian heyday, decoupage experienced a gradual decline in popularity. A few devotees, most notably Hiram Manning in the USA, made valiant attempts to revive the craft before and after the Second World War. But it took the technical innovations of the late twentieth century, such as fast-drying varnishes and the photocopying machine, to make decoupage more accessible and popular than ever.

Mary Delany's 'Arabian Star of Bethlehem' (above) and 'Asphodil Lily' (left). Every petal, leaf and stamen is formed from layer upon layer of coloured paper pieces.

The current practice of decoupage divides roughly into two schools of thought. There are those who prefer to use ready-coloured materials, ransacking wallpaper designs, wrapping papers and magazine illustrations for juicily-coloured motifs to cut out. Others prefer to start with black-and-white printed motifs, colouring these according to personal taste. The first approach resembles the Victorian 'scrap' technique – glossily gorgeous but a touch predictable. The second is closer in spirit and effect to the Venetian *arte povera*, and allows more scope for individual interpretation. What we have tried to do in this book is to provide any *aficionado* with enough printed material of quality and variety to work innumerable transformations, plus sufficient practical advice to make it user-friendly, and get you going with the scissors or the scalpel!

TOOLS & MATERIALS

1. Wet-and-dry abrasive paper
2. Metal primer 3. Acrylic gesso
4. Large scissors 5. Artists' acrylic paints
6. Curved manicure scissors 7. PVA glue
8. Paintbrushes 9. Wallpaper paste
10. Finger bowl and natural sponge
11. Clear satin varnish 12. Acrylic varnish
13. Tinted varnish 14. Beeswax 15. Wire wool
16., 17. and 18. Craquelure varnishes 19. Surgical gloves
20. Soft cloth 21. Artists' tube oil paints
22. Pages from the source section (see pp. 33–96)
23. Tinted motifs 24. Coloured pencils
25. Watercolour inks

One of the factors that makes decoupage so accessible – to beginners, especially – is that no special tools or equipment are required to carry out projects. You'll probably find that you already own several, if not all, of the items listed in this section. The most pivotal decoupage tool – a pair of scissors – is common to most households, and varnishes, sandpaper and paintbrushes often lurk in cupboards under the stairs or in makeshift tool-kits. You can use ordinary coloured pencils to tint motifs, and standard emulsions as base paints. All the items listed here can be picked up at DIY, hardware or artists' supply stores (see Suppliers, p. 32), and none is costly.

The right tool can make a job easier, but there is no reason to buy everything in our picture at one go. The essentials, needed for all the decoupage projects in this book, are listed under 'Basic Equipment' on p. 11. Any additional equipment required is listed on a project by project basis.

Source Material

The source section (see pp. 33–96) includes hundreds of ready-to-use, black-and-white designs. The pages are perforated for easy removal; just pull them out and either photocopy or snip out your favourite motifs. Sourcebooks take the hard work out of decoupage, but if you enjoy hunting around for ready-coloured, unusual or contemporary motifs, almost any type of printed material – from magazines and newspapers, to wrapping paper or greetings cards – can be raided for suitable images.

Cutting Tools

The most important piece of decoupage equipment is your cutting tool, or tools. A large pair of scissors is handy for rough – and speedy – cutting out. For finer work, some people swear by the best quality, curved manicure scissors, finely pointed to let you puncture the paper on an 'inside' cut without tearing. Others are more comfortable with a slim craft knife, or scalpel, and a box of refill blades. Cutting paper blunts a sharp edge quickly, so replacement blades are useful. On the other hand, you will also need a pair of pliers to extract used blades and possibly a cutting mat to work on. Consider the safety aspect, too: always handle scalpels with care, and keep out of the reach of children.

Preparing Surfaces

To look professional, decoupage should be applied to a well-prepared surface. Bare wood, papier mâché, metal and MDF (medium-density fibreboard) may only need rubbing down with abrasive paper, to smooth off roughness, followed by the appropriate primer and base paint. But a junk buy covered in old paint or varnish is best stripped down to the wood. Do this with the appropriate stripper, wearing gloves and working out-of-doors if possible. Brush stripper on as directed and leave paint or varnish to soften. Then, working in the direction of the wood grain, use a scraper to strip off the layers, followed by pads of medium-to-coarse wire wool to clean back to bare wood. Finish by sanding thoroughly. Cracks, knotholes and unsightly blemishes should be filled with wood filler. Fill 'proud', allow to dry, then sand flat.

Priming is important if your finished piece is to look really sleek. Use acrylic gesso or acrylic primer on bare wood. Both dry fast, and build up a flawless surface if you apply several coats and sand smooth in between. On metal, a metal primer will encourage paint to bond well, and will discourage rust. MDF should be sealed first with orange shellac (button polish) before priming with gesso, because it is important to stop moisture entering the 'end grain' (the cut sides).

Supply yourself with several grades of abrasive papers, from coarse to fine, for rubbing back wood, and polishing primer to porcelain smoothness. Always rub back in the direction of the wood grain, never against it. Wet-and-dry paper, used with care, is nifty for smoothing paint and varnishes. Dipping the paper in water, then lightly smearing it with soap, lubricates the cutting action and helps prevent you removing too much paint or varnish at a time. Soft- and medium-grade wire (steel) wool is also good for smoothing, but dust very carefully afterwards to clear off tiny filaments.

Paints

Paint Magic Woodwash colours (see Suppliers, p. 32), work well as base paints. They cover well, dry fast and sand back to a fine close surface. Plaka acrylic colours are also excellent, but more expensive. Emulsion paints can be substituted, too.

Artists' acrylic colours, in tubes or pots, are ideal for colouring in your images because once acrylic colours dry they are permanent. Before use, they should be diluted to transparency with water. Avoid using colours opaquely because heavy colour will mask the printed detail of your images. Watercolour inks and coloured pencils can also be used, for extra softness of colour. At least three watercolour brushes, one fine, one medium and one thick, preferably sable, are needed for brushing colour on neatly. Wash out carefully after use.

Print Sealers and Adhesives

PVA glue, diluted with water (1 part PVA to 2 parts water), is invaluable for 'sealing' decoupage motifs prior to cutting out. It will prevent paper from stretching, and ink from smudging. Swab on lightly with a soft brush. When the paper has dried out it may look a little wrinkled, but don't worry: once the motifs are pasted down they will appear perfectly flat. For pasting down, ordinary wallpaper paste is ideal, drying slowly enough to let you slide motifs around experimentally, and leaving no trace of stickiness or discolouration. A small soft sponge, squeezed out in water till moist, is useful for wiping up any paste that has leaked onto base paint.

Varnishes

Varnishing is very much the secret of professional-looking decoupage. Old pieces were varnished up to thirty or forty times to produce surfaces of glassy smoothness, but such perfectionism is not current practice. Generally speaking, between five and twelve coats are ample. If even this sounds daunting, remember that modern varnishes dry very quickly, especially the acrylic ones.

Your choice of varnish will depend on the piece. Purely decorative pieces can be finished entirely in acrylic varnish, fast drying and non-yellowing, rubbed back after the first three or four coats, and then again after each successive one. On pieces needing tougher protection, the last few coats should generally be clear polyurethane. This yellows slightly in time, though less if you thin it with 10 per cent white spirit, but a little yellowing has an attractive 'antiquing' effect.

Bleached shellac (white polish) is spirit based, quick drying and very glossy. It adds a certain glow and richness to colours, characteristic of eighteenth-century pieces. As shellac is thin, extra care is needed when rubbing down not to cut through to the paint.

Always leave varnishes to dry hard, overnight where possible, and apply with a fine soft brush, brushing each new coat at right angles to the one before to minimize brushmarks. Don't skimp on the rubbing back, because this not only clears off any grit or hairs that might have become embedded in the varnish, but compacts the surface and gives the work a fine, solid look.

Special Finishes

A craquelure (cracked) finish is achieved by applying a fast-drying, water-based varnish over a slower-drying, oil-based one. When these two varnishes, sold as a pack, react together, they produce a fascinatingly 'crazed' surface which can be accentuated with oil paint to add instant age to a decoupage piece. Some brands of craquelure now offer a choice of either fine or large cracks, so you can choose the most appropriate finish for your decoupage.

Waxes

Some people like to add a final 'sheen' to their finished decoupaged pieces by polishing with beeswax, or even with ordinary shoe polish. Rub in with a soft cloth. Leave to dry for a few hours before polishing off.

Odds and Ends

Thin surgical gloves are handy for messy jobs like stripping paint, or sanding. Rags, preferably soft cotton, are always useful, as are clean jars with lids, sheets of old newspaper and palettes for mixing paints. A small bowl of water will keep sponges moist and fingers clean.

BASIC EQUIPMENT

The following is a list of equipment common to all the projects in this book. Start by assembling this small 'kit', then build up your collection of paints and varnishes as you progress.

Small curved manicure scissors or scalpel,
for fine cutting
Larger scissors, for rough cutting
Brushes for sealing, painting, gluing and varnishing
Wallpaper paste
PVA glue
Natural sponge
Finger bowl and water
Soft rags

PHOTOCOPYING

There can be no doubt that the availability and cost-effectiveness of photocopying has given decoupage a tremendous boost. Instead of chopping up sourcebooks for the image that takes your fancy, you can get the page – or even just the image – reproduced in seconds, and with perfect accuracy. Few individuals will have their own photocopying equipment, though anyone thinking of decoupage as a paying sideline would be well advised to investigate costs. For the occasional project, having images photocopied for you works out very reasonably; the days of hunting for antique prints and cutting them up guiltily are long gone.

Enlarging and Reducing Images

Most small towns now have at least one studio or shop where you can have work copied to your specifications. Large images can be reduced by 50 per cent, and small images magnified by anything up to 400 per cent. Modern colour copiers offer many more sophisticated options, such as creating 'negative', white-on-black images, or making double-sided colour copies, though for the majority of decoupage projects, you will probably find that re-sizing is the facility you want to use most often.

Enlarging and reducing images by trial and error, until you arrive at the perfect fit for your box, vase or piece of furniture, can be costly. If you can, work out the exact magnification required before you have your motifs copied, by applying the formula:

$$\frac{\textit{The size you would like the image to be}}{\textit{The size of the original}} \times 100$$

For example, to enlarge a motif that measures 7 cm (3 in) in length to fit a box just over 20 cm (8 in) long, you would need a magnification of 285 % ($20 \div 7 \times 100 = 285$).

Very large designs require a slightly different approach, however. In an ideal world, your local photocopying shop will have facilities to enlarge to A0 size – the largest paper size on top-of-the-range photocopiers. It's more likely, however, that A2 or A3 will be the only options available to you. If you want to transform a small printed image into a gigantic one, like the tiger design used for our dummy board (see p. 19, and p. 58 of the source section), you may have to reproduce the image in sections. First, copy your motif onto A3 paper, at the maximum enlargement that will fit on the page. To arrive at a considerably larger blow-up, divide the A3 photocopy into 6 sections (see right). Copy each section onto A3 paper, again at the maximum enlargement to fit. The resulting 'jigsaw' pieces, carefully cut out using a ruler and scalpel, fit together to make a perfectly detailed and precise enlargement of the original. With accurate pasting down, the pieces will look just like one continuous image, and layers of varnish will disguise the joins.

The same technique was used to enlarge the classical figures on the Grecian Screen (see pp. 30–1), though the original motifs differed slightly in size and needed standardizing before we began.

Larger images achieved in this way can be transformed into dummy or chimney boards very simply. Paste down your pieces with wallpaper paste onto a piece of MDF large enough to accommodate your image. Leave to dry, then cut around the image with a jigsaw. Use fine-grade abrasive paper to smooth off around the edges and finish by tinting, sealing and varnishing. Hang your finished piece on the wall, or attach to a simple wooden stand.

Colour Copying

Colour copiers introduce another attractive possibility. The coloured butterflies used for our gift boxes (see pp. 28–9) began as black-and-white images. Programming the machine to copy these in mauve resulted in a whole different breed of coloured butterflies, at the press of a button. Not all the images on each sheet have to be the same colour, incidentally. The machine can be programmed to give several colours per sheet, if you are in an experimental mood.

Colour copying can be expensive, though, so plan to get the maximum number of images out of each sheet. Bear in mind that not all photocopying outlets have colour laser copiers, so check first to find out what options are available to you.

Tips and Ideas

Modern photocopiers can enlarge without distortion or loss of detail. You may notice, however, if you have a great deal of photocopying done, that the ink intensity can vary quite considerably, rendering some copies a rich black and white and others a medium grey. This usually occurs when the machine ink is running out over a day's use, so try to get all your copying done in one batch.

For those on a tight budget, there are ways to cut photocopying costs. If one assemblage of designs, collected from different pages in this book, is one you feel you want to repeat often, you can cut and paste down the photocopied images onto a standard A3 sheet and have it copied as many times as you need.

Linework and engravings photocopy better than mezzotints, where the dark areas are made up of an infinity of black dots. Heavy magnification of these dots will tend to give a spotty, though still recognizable, image.

Original Size

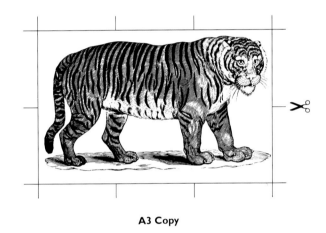

A3 Copy

Enlarging an image (from top to bottom):

1. Enlarge the motif onto A3 paper

2. Cut into six sections and enlarge each to A3 size

3. Fit together to form one continuous image

FANCY FRAMES

Picture frames are the ideal subjects for decoupage. Their strict shape encourages the imagination: you can smother the frame with images, or work on the less-is-more principle, dotting them here and there as your inner eye dictates. You can 'theme' a decoupage frame to suit its contents: sweetly pretty florals for a snap of granny as a girl, cupids for a loving couple, insects and creepy-crawlies for a naughty boy.

Simple new wood frames are also cheap, and easy to prepare for decoupage. Smooth rough patches with medium-grade abrasive paper, fill any gaping cracks with wood filler, allow to dry, then sand flat. Apply a couple of coats of acrylic gesso, sanding down between coats, then paint with your chosen base colour.

Final varnishing is less important with purely decorative items like frames, as they won't be subject to wear and tear. Craquelure – the antiquing 'crazed' finish shown on the seashell frame in our step-by-step photographs – is a purely optional finish, but is ideal for giving motifs a gentle, rather than crisply graphic, look.

YOU WILL NEED

Basic equipment (see p. 11)
Wooden picture frame
Fish and seashell motifs (see pp. 52–5)
Blu-Tack
Acrylic varnish
'Fine-crack' acrylic craquelure
Raw Umber artists' tube oil colour

1 Assemble your chosen motifs. You can either pull pages of designs straight from the source section (see pp. 33–96), or photocopy your favourite motifs onto ordinary photocopy paper. Coat the entire sheet you want to use with a thin layer of diluted PVA glue (1 part PVA to 2 parts water), brushed on smoothly. This will prevent photocopying ink from smudging, and toughen flimsy photocopy paper.

2 When the diluted PVA glue has dried (this will take about 20 minutes), roughly cut out the motifs with a large pair of scissors, then carefully snip out the details using sharp manicure scissors. Scalpels are ideal for speeding up fiddly cutting, but they should always be used with extreme care.

3 Assemble the cut-outs and try them out for effect on the prepared frame. This is the fun, creative part, and worth spending some time over. As a rule, asymmetric arrangements, or those where motifs bend round the sides, tend to look more interesting than regimented designs. Experiment by temporarily attaching the cut-outs around the frame with Blu-Tack. Mark their final positions with a pencil, if it helps.

4 Coat the whole frame with a thin layer of wallpaper paste. This doesn't dry immediately and so keeps the surface 'open' when you come to position the cut-outs, allowing you to slide them around easily. Next, coat the motifs on the back, one by one, with the same paste.

5 Brush the paste out smoothly. Never slop it on – a thin coat is enough! Begin positioning your motifs in the pre-arranged order. Smooth out with the brush, then with a soft rag, pressing out air bubbles. It's best to start from the centre of the motif and work outwards.

6 When quite dry (wait a couple of hours), the decoupaged frame should be wiped over gently with a damp soft sponge to clear paste from the base paint. Though not strictly necessary you might like to seal the work, when dry, with a first coat of acrylic varnish.

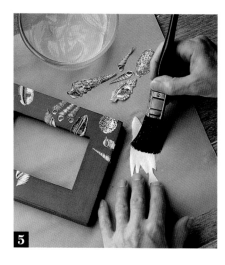

7 Wait about half an hour, until your sealing coat of acrylic varnish is dry, then brush the first, slow-drying coat of craquelure over the entire frame. If this is too thick and sticky to apply, don't be tempted to add water – just dampen your brush with a little water before dipping it into the craquelure. It should now brush out more smoothly and evenly. Make sure you have not missed any areas by squinting along the frame in a bright light – the varnish will look wet and shiny. Leave for about 20 minutes, until the frame feels dry to the touch, but just tacky when pressed with a finger.

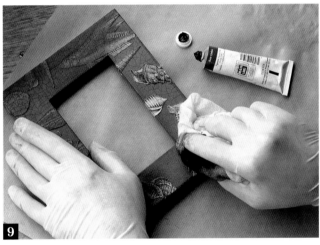

8 Now apply the second, fast-drying coat of craquelure, to cover the first completely. (Again, make sure that the whole surface of the frame has been coated. Any areas that you miss will still be tacky when you rub in the oil paint, and will show up as dark blotches.) As this coat dries it will 'craze' the slower-drying coat beneath. As both coats are transparent, don't expect dramatic results. If you hold the frame to the light you will notice fine cracks appearing over the whole surface. The best policy is to set the piece aside overnight now, so all cracking can be completed naturally.

9 The exciting stage has been reached. Wearing rubber gloves, dip a soft rag into a little artists' tube oil colour – Raw Umber or Burnt Umber are the usual choices, both good 'dirtying' shades – and rub paint over the entire surface liberally. Don't make the mistake of using artists' acrylic colour – this just leaves an ugly smear. Leave to settle for a few minutes, then go over with a clean soft rag. You will find the dark oil colour settles into the 'cracks', showing them up for the first time as an intricate web of fine lines. Don't rub too much, though, or you will clear most of the oil colour from the rest

of the surface. If you missed any areas with the second coat of varnish, dark patches may begin to show up on your frame. If this happens, soak a cotton wool bud in white spirit and gently rub over the area to dissolve the paint. Unfortunately, this may also dissolve the cracks, so work carefully. Leave for a day or two for the oil colour to harden, then finish with as many coats of acrylic varnish as you fancy giving your first masterpiece. Two or three coats of acrylic varnish will be ample to give a smooth solid surface that can be dusted or wiped down from time to time.

JUNGLE FEVER

Chunky chests and blanket boxes are the greatest fun to decorate with decoupage. We felt that this one, destined to be a toy box, should be a riot of colour and interest, evoking the jolly 'scrap work' beloved of Victorian nurseries. Colouring the motifs takes time, but with coloured pencils, as shown, it is therapeutic and enjoyable to do. Don't be too finicky and realistic with the colours; brightness is all. And don't forget the inside – paint it a contrasting colour and paste a zebra or lobster on the under lid as a surprise.

The near-life-size tiger dummy board standing guard over the box is a fun extra (see pp. 12–13). Don't be put off by the sheer scale of it. It's a perfect project for tiny helpers, as larger designs call for less fiddly, precise colouring in.

A new box in pristine condition only needs a light sanding to prepare it for painting, but old chests may require stripping down first (see p. 10) and sanding, followed by two or three coats of acrylic primer. Give the primed box two coats of base paint, smooth lightly and seal with a coat of acrylic varnish.

YOU WILL NEED

Basic equipment (see p. 11)
Wooden chest or large box
Coloured pencils
Animal, fish and insect motifs (see pp. 50–61)
Acrylic varnish
Polyurethane varnish
Fine wire wool
Wet-and-dry abrasive paper

1

1 Use coloured pencils, with nicely sharpened points, to colour in your menagerie of motifs. Seal with diluted PVA glue (see p. 15) and let dry before cutting out. Lay out the coloured pieces roughly to form your design, then coat the back of the motifs and the box side or top with wallpaper paste. Apply the motifs – you will be able to slide them about for several minutes till the arrangement suits. The odd tear can be invisibly mended at this stage. Smooth pieces down, first with the paste brush, then with a soft cloth. When all is dry, wipe off excess paste with a damp sponge.

2 Leave the box to dry overnight, then apply a few coats of fast-drying acrylic varnish to 'fix' your work. Toy boxes need tough sealing, so finish up with several layers of clear polyurethane varnish, rubbing down after the first coat with fine wire wool (dusting off meticulously) and subsequent coats with wet-and-dry abrasive paper lubricated with water and a smear of soap. Wipe off each time. A useful varnishing tip is to dilute the first coats of polyurethane varnish (10 parts varnish to 1 part white spirit) because this makes it brush out more smoothly and discolour less in time.

OAK-LEAF BOX

These handsome wooden boxes were primed, coloured with acrylic paints in shades of maize, chestnut and green, and adorned with flowers and autumn fruits. They were the most highly varnished of all our projects – fifteen coats of acrylic varnish – and this has given them an almost lacquer-like smoothness.

YOU WILL NEED

Basic equipment (see p. 11)
Wooden box
Oak leaf motifs (see p. 38)
Yellow and green acrylic artists' colours
Pencil
Scalpel
Ruler or set square
'Large-crack' acrylic craquelure
Raw Umber artists' tube oil colour
Medium-grade abrasive paper
Matt acrylic varnish

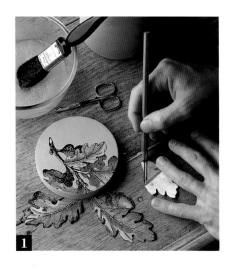

1

1 Decorating round lidded boxes, with motifs spilling over from the tops to the sides, involves some fiddly piecing to make sure the flat paper shapes line up correctly along the curved rim. Motifs have to be cut and 'invisibly' joined at the rim, because paper does not curve naturally. Don't worry about the joins showing up on your finished piece – the many coats of varnish will render them completely invisible.

Tint your motifs with thinned acrylic artists' colours in suitably autumnal hues. Seal with diluted PVA glue (see p. 15), then paste down on the lid of a box with wallpaper paste, and slice off along the curving rim with scissors or a scalpel. A twin of the truncated oak leaf is here being marked for cutting and joining to the motif on the lid.

2 Make pencil marks to determine where to cut the leaf again round the bottom of the lid, leaving a narrow strip to paste down. Fiddly as this may seem it is worth the trouble involved to achieve a smooth flow of pattern around the boxes. Provide yourself with a few spares when tackling this kind of couturier snipping, then if your measurements slip up, replacements are to hand.

3 Line up the last segment of oak leaf to follow on from the lid, and paste down. Make sure motifs are thoroughly taut when pasting on boxes, because these will get a lot of handling. However, multi-varnishing goes some way towards keeping everything in place.

4 Next, apply 'large-crack' craquelure (see p. 17) to give the box an impressively crazed finish. When dry, rub the 'antiquing' oil tube colour, Raw Umber, over the entire surface with a soft rag, so that the colour settles into the cracks and dramatizes the craquelure. Leave to dry off for a day or two, then varnish repeatedly with matt acrylic varnish, rubbing down after the first two or three coats with medium-grade abrasive paper.

TOPPING TABLE

This whimsical table top, with its *faux* cutlery decoration, is basically a sturdy square of plywood. To arrive at a good, smooth surface for decoupage, sand thoroughly with medium-grade abrasive paper, then apply three coats of acrylic primer, rubbed down in between. It is important to prime both sides of the board, to prevent warping. Paint the square with white undercoat, used as a top coat for its chalky finish, and, when dry, seal with clear acrylic varnish.

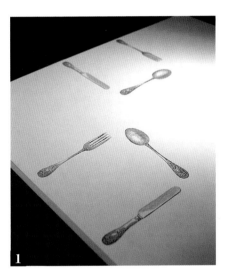

1 First, prime and prepare the plywood (see above). Seal the paper 'cutlery' with diluted PVA glue (see p. 15). Lay out at measured intervals, one 'setting' per side. Use a real dinner plate to get a feel for the correct spacing.

2 Paste down your first setting with wallpaper paste, then use a ruler to match the others up to it. But don't get too mathematical about it; this is a project to have fun with. We added a pretty cruet, four wine glasses and a butterfly – for their shape as much as their appropriateness. An immaculate look is essential to this sort of graphic decoration, so varnish thoroughly with clear acrylic varnish, smoothing down between coats.

1 Wipe metal objects over with a rag dampened with white spirit to remove any traces of rust remover and/or greasy fingermarks. Then use a standard paintbrush to give the surfaces a coat of metal primer. Don't be tempted to skip this stage. Metal primer bonds well with metal surfaces and also discourages further rusting. It is well worth giving metal this extra protection because rust will eventually stain and corrode its way through any paint surface that is applied on top.

Apply the primer and leave to dry. For a super-smooth final finish it may be best to rub down at this stage with wet-and-dry paper (used dry) and re-coat. Metal needs to be smoothly finished for successful decoupage.

When the primer has dried, cover with grey-green acrylic paint (we used Paint Magic's Gustavian Green Woodwash). Again, two coats may be needed to completely cover the primer.

2 Seal black-and-white seashell motifs with diluted PVA glue (see p. 15). Cut them out, then paste down with wallpaper paste, starting with the larger shells round the top of the vase and finishing up with narrow, pointed ones at the bottom. Wallpaper paste dries slowly and so allows plenty of time for re-positioning motifs.

SEASHELL VASE

3 When the wallpaper paste has dried, finish off the vase with 'fine-crack' craquelure, following the method given on p. 17, but replacing the 'dirtying' Raw Umber colour with Cobalt Violet artists' tube oil colour. As well as giving the shells a delicate pinky tinge, this colour makes an attractive contrast to the grey-green base paint.

After 24 hours, varnish with matt or eggshell acrylic varnish. Several coats will look better than one, and a light rub down with wet-and-dry abrasive paper (used wet) will bring the piece up to a fine smooth finish.

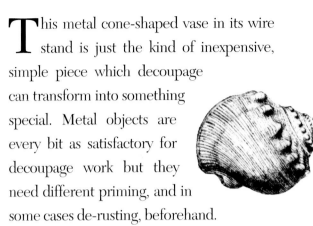

This metal cone-shaped vase in its wire stand is just the kind of inexpensive, simple piece which decoupage can transform into something special. Metal objects are every bit as satisfactory for decoupage work but they need different priming, and in some cases de-rusting, beforehand.

This piece was fashioned from new metal so there was no flaky paint or rust patches to worry about. An old metal box or trunk, on the other hand, may well present more problems. Rust is best treated with a proprietary rust remover applied according to directions. When the preparation has softened the old rust, rub the surface back to sound metal with wire wool pads. If you have an electric drill, the wire brush attachment will clean off rust more satisfactorily still. Any remaining flaky paint can be removed with wet-and-dry abrasive paper rubbed briskly over the area. Wipe thoroughly, then coat the whole piece with metal primer.

YOU WILL NEED

Basic equipment (see p. 11)
Metal vase
White spirit
Metal primer
Grey-green acrylic paint
Seashell motifs (see pp. 52–5)
'Fine-crack' acrylic craquelure
Cobalt Violet artists' tube oil colour
Matt or eggshell acrylic varnish
Wet-and-dry abrasive paper

PROJECT 6

STRAWBERRY BOWL

Glass is an unusual but attractive choice for decoupage treatment. The vivid strawberry motifs here are applied to the underside of the bowl, and backed with a coat of off-white oil paint, so that the colours seen through the thickness of the glass gain a jewel-like brilliance. This way there is no risk of toxic content in the paint affecting food in the bowl itself. Before and after use, simply rinse out the inside of the bowl and polish dry with a soft cloth.

Glass kitchenware is cheap and sturdy. This treatment upgrades it visually into the luxury class. Imagine a set of matching glass plates, each with its succulent strawberry appliqué on the base. Not dishwasher-proof, perhaps, but a stunning feast for the eye, worth going to a little extra trouble for.

Glass needs no special preparation for decoupage work; just make sure all surfaces are clean and dry before starting work. If the idea of tinting several motifs by hand doesn't appeal, you can save time by colouring in one motif and using a colour copier to reproduce a sheet of strawberries in mouthwatering detail.

YOU WILL NEED

Basic equipment (see p. 11)
Glass bowl
Strawberry motifs (see p. 44)
Green, yellow and red watercolour paints
Spray print fixative
Water-soluble marker pen
Off-white and green oil-based paints

1 Colour in the strawberry motifs with watercolour paints; we worked with bright, rather than subtle, shades of red and leaf-green, and added vivid yellow highlights. It's best not to use PVA glue to seal prints that have been tinted with watercolours – being water-based itself, it can make colours run. Instead, when the motifs have dried, seal them with a spray print fixative (this is best done out-of-doors, if possible. If not, make sure the room you are working in is well ventilated). Leave to dry again before carefully cutting out. Next, work out the positioning of the strawberries, moving

the motifs around behind the glass. You might find it helps to mark the position of each strawberry on the top surface of the glass with water-soluble marker pen. Apply PVA glue to the *front* of the motifs with a small soft brush.

2 Attach the strawberries one by one, smoothing down with a soft rag. Here, some of the motifs have been attached at the top of the bowl, and their overlapping edges trimmed with a craft knife. Leave to dry out thoroughly. PVA glue looks milky to begin with but don't worry; it dries crystal clear.

3 When all the strawberries are firmly attached, give the outside of the bowl a couple of coats of off-white oil paint. Take extra care when painting near the rim. You might find it easier to place the bowl upside down on several sheets of newspaper or kitchen paper first, to prevent any of the paint leaking over the rim. Leave to dry, then apply green oil paint (we chose a shade that matched the strawberry stalks) over the off-white paint in four or five coats or until the raised edges of the motifs are no longer visible. Any pen marks on the inside of the bowl can be easily removed with a damp cloth.

BUTTERFLIES

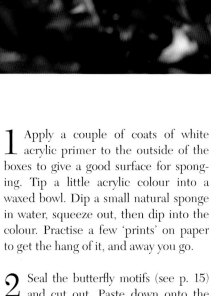

These butterfly gift boxes (right) feature no fewer than three special effects. First, sponging, to give an interesting background for decoupage. Next, we processed a black-and-white sheet of butterflies through a colour photo-copier to give mauve-tinted butterflies at the press of a button (see p. 13). Lastly, the box was 'laminated' with a sheet of white tissue paper, to give a pretty, soft-focus look to the decoration.

Colour copying may not be the cheapest of options, but a couple of sheets of coloured butter-flies will provide ample material for a few extras, such as our gift tags and simple mobile.

YOU WILL NEED

Basic equipment (see p. 11)
Cardboard boxes
White acrylic primer
Blue acrylic paint
Butterfly motifs (see pp. 50–1), photocopied in mauve
White tissue paper

1

2

1 Apply a couple of coats of white acrylic primer to the outside of the boxes to give a good surface for spong-ing. Tip a little acrylic colour into a waxed bowl. Dip a small natural sponge in water, squeeze out, then dip into the colour. Practise a few 'prints' on paper to get the hang of it, and away you go.

2 Seal the butterfly motifs (see p. 15) and cut out. Paste down onto the boxes with wallpaper paste. When dry, coat box surfaces thinly with wallpaper paste. Cut two pieces of tissue to fit the box and the lid, leaving extra to tuck in

round the edges. Lay the first piece out over the box lid then use a soft brush, dampened with paste, to spread it out smooth and taut, starting in the middle and working outwards. Nick paper to fit round the corners without overlaps, then take the tissue round the sides, pulling it taut, and paste down on the inside. Coat the box in the same way.

Turn leftover butterflies into gift tags. Paste onto thin card with wallpaper paste. Cut out, then use a scalpel to make two tiny cuts in the middle of each butterfly. Loop a strip of ribbon down through the first 'slot', and back up through the second.

3 To make a mobile, you will need 'double-sided' butterflies, so, when copying, allow two prints per image. Colour copiers can also be programmed to photocopy more than one colour on the same sheet (see p. 13); try blue, crimson, gold and green. Use the thickest photocopying paper available, for added durability. Roughly cut out one of the butterflies, then its twin image. Glue the two images together with a thin coat of wallpaper paste – holding the paper up to the light will help you to see the outlines of the butterflies more clearly – then cut out neatly.

4 Fold each butterfly in half, using a ruler to make a sharp central crease. Make a tiny hole with a pin directly in the middle of the crease, and feed through a short length of fine soft wire, bending the wire back underneath the butterfly, so that it runs parallel to the tail. Secure with clear adhesive tape. At the top of the wire, make a tiny loop. Thread thin twine through the loops and attach the butterflies to a wood or wire cruciform frame. Balance problems can be adjusted with a blob of Blu-Tack. Remember that wire is sharp, so don't hang the mobile within the reach of small children.

GRECIAN SCREEN

Decoupage can be grand as well as pretty. Here, a trio of classical figures immediately strikes a dignified note, and the obvious location for them had to be a decorative folding screen, one panel per deity. A clear blue background suggested a Greek sky, and a strong but simple arched border acted as a frame. The splendid figures, with their flowing draperies and noble poses, did the rest.

The MDF panels that make up our screen were sanded, shellacked, primed, and given two coats of blue base paint, lightly rubbed down between coats for extra smoothness. A first sealing coat of acrylic varnish at this stage is purely optional but helps prevent marks and scratches as you work.

YOU WILL NEED

Basic equipment (see p. 11)
MDF or wooden screen
Classical figures (see pp. 82–3)
Decorative border (see pp. 90–5)
Set square and/or steel rule
Scalpel
Pencil or chalk
Matt acrylic
varnish

1 Enlarge each motif following the method on pp. 12–13. You will end up with six equal sections, which, when pasted togther, add up to a complete image, just under half life-size. Neatly cut away the white margins from around the six sections with a scalpel and steel rule. The images can be cut out with the same scalpel or with the usual curved scissors. Seal with diluted PVA glue before or after cutting out.

2 Brush wallpaper paste over the screen as well as on the back of the images, to allow you to slide them about till the 'jigsaw' pieces join up neatly. Make sure the images line up along the bottom of the panels, and are properly centered.

3 Pencil or chalk a guideline for pasting the border round each panel. To arrive at the arched border, trace the arch curve onto paper, cut and overlap segments of the border to mimic the curve exactly, then photocopy this 'paste-up' three times. The border motif looks intricate but is actually a smooth straightforward cut. Use a set square to help you achieve the neatly mitered corner. Finish with matt acrylic varnish.

SUPPLIERS

UNITED KINGDOM

J W Bollom
121 South Liberty Lane, Ashton Vale, Bristol
Tel: 0272 665151
Varnishes, craquelure, gilding materials, glues, shellac, gesso, artists' oil paints, brushes. Delivery service from 8 nationwide branches.

Cornelisson and Son
105 Great Russell Street, London WC1B 3LX
Tel: 0171 636 1045
Fax: 0171 636 3655
A full range of decoupage tools and materials. Mail order.

The Dover Bookshop
18 Earlham Street, London WC2H 9LN
Tel: 0171 836 2111
Fax: 0171 836 1603
Decoupage sourcebooks. Catalogue available. Mail order.

Fiddes and Sons
Florence Works, Bridley Road, Cardiff
Tel: 01222 340323
Varnishes, craquelure, glues, shellac, emulsion paints, brushes, metal primer. Mail order.

W Habberley Meadows
5 Saxon Way, Chelmsley Wood, Birmingham B37 5AY
Tel: 0121 770 2905
A full range of tools and materials.

A S Handover
Angel Yard, Highgate High Street, London N6 5JU
Tel: 0181 340 0665
Cutting tools, varnishes, craquelure, gilding materials, glues, gesso, shellac, artists' paints, watercolours. Mail order.

John T Keep and Sons
15 Theobalds Road, London WC1X 8SL
Tel: 0171 242 7578
Cutting tools, varnishes, gilt cream, glues, shellac, emulsion paints, artists' oil paints, brushes, metal primer.

London Graphic Centre
107-115 Long Acre London WC2E 9NT
Tel: 0171 240 0095
A large range of artists' materials, including acrylic and oil paints, paintbrushes and gilding materials.

E Milner
Glanville Road, Cowley, Oxford OX4 2DB
Tel: 0865 718171
Cutting tools, varnishes, craquelure, gilding materials, glues, shellac, gesso, emulsions, brushes. Mail order.

John Myland Ltd
80 Norwood High Street, London SE27 9NW
Tel: 0181 670 9161
Varnishes, crackle glaze, glues, gilt cream, shellac, gesso, emulsion paints, brushes, Mail order.

John Oliver Paints & Wallpapers
33 Pembridge Road London W11 3HG
Tel: 0171 221 6466
Emulsion paints. Mail order.

Paint Magic
116 Sheen Road, Richmond, Surrey TW9 1UR
Tel: 0181 940 5503
Tools, books, motifs, materials, Paint Magic paints.

E Ploton Ltd
273 Archway Road, London N6 5AA
Tel: 0181 348 0315
Cutting tools, varnishes, craquelure, gilding materials, shellac, gesso, artists' paints, watercolours, brushes. Mail order, except for inflammable or toxic items.

Stuart Stevenson
68 Clerkenwell Road, London EC1
Tel: 0171 253 1693
Cutting tools, varnishes, craquelure, gilding materials, glues, shellac, gesso, artists' paints, watercolours, brushes, metal primer. Mail order.

AUSTRALIA

The Folk Art Studio
200 Pittwater Road, Manly, NSW 2095
Tel: 02 977 7091
A full range of decoupage tools and materials.

Handworks Supplies
121 Commercial Road, Prahan, Victoria 3181
Tel: 03 820 8399
Stockists of general art supplies.

Janet's Art Supplies and Art Books
145 Victoria Avenue, Chatswood 2067, Sydney
Tel: 02 417 8572
Decoupage kits and 'scraps'.

Paper 'N' Things
88 Union Street, Armadale, Victoria 3143
Tel: 03 576 0223
A full range of decoupage materials.

CANADA

Coast Decorating Centre
4464 Main Street, Vancouver, BC, VSV 3R3
Tel: 604 872 5275
Brushes and decorating tools, natural sponges, glazes, paints.

Day's Painting Supplies
10733 104 Avenue, Edmonton, AB, T5J 3K1
Tel: 403 426 4848

Natural sponges, glazes and special paints.

Maiwa Supplies
6-1666 Johnston Street, Vancouver, BC, V6H 3S2
Tel: 604 669 3939
Decoupage materials.

Mona Lisa Artists' Materials
1518 7th Street SW Calgary, AB, T2R 1A7
Tel: 403 228 3618
A wide range of decoupage and artists' materials.

Nautilus Arts & Crafts Inc
6057 Kingston Road, Westhill, ON, M1C 1K5
Tel: 416 284 1171
Prints and decoupage materials.

New York Paint & Wallpaper
1704 Clair Avenue, West Toronto, ON, M6N 1J1
Tel: 416 656 2223
A full range of decorating supplies, including sea sponges and glazes.

Paint Magic
101, 1019 17th Avenue, SW, Calgary, AB, T2T OA7
Tel: 403 245 6866
Stockists of a full range of Paint Magic paints, plus decoupage prints, books, tools and materials.

Western Paint and Wallcovering Co Ltd
521 Hargrave Street, Winnipeg, MB, R3A OY1
Tel: 204 942 7271
Paints and glazes.

White Rose
4400 Dufferin Street, North York, ON, M3H 5R9
Tel: 416 663 4172
Decoupage tools and materials.

SOUTH AFRICA
The following outlets supply a wide range of decoupage and artists' tools and materials.

Art Book Centre
Sandton Place, Corner of Elizabeth & 10th Street, Parkmore, Johannesburg
Tel: 011 8835304

Barney's Paint Centre
Fourways Shopping Centre, Bryanston, Johannesburg
Tel: 011 4656490

Crafty Supplies
32 Main Road, Claremont Cape
Tel: 021 610286

P W Story (Pty) Ltd
18 Foundry Lane, Durban
Tel: 031 3061224

Wardkiss Homecare DIY Superstores
Blue Route Shopping Centre, PO Box 30094, Tokai Cape
Tel: 021 725000

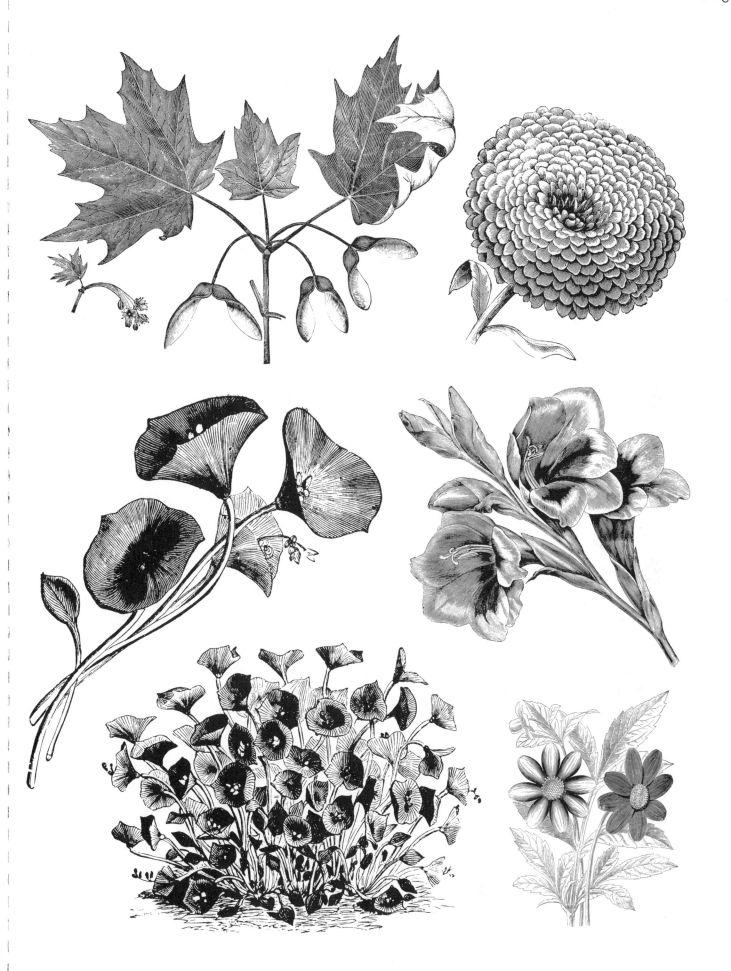

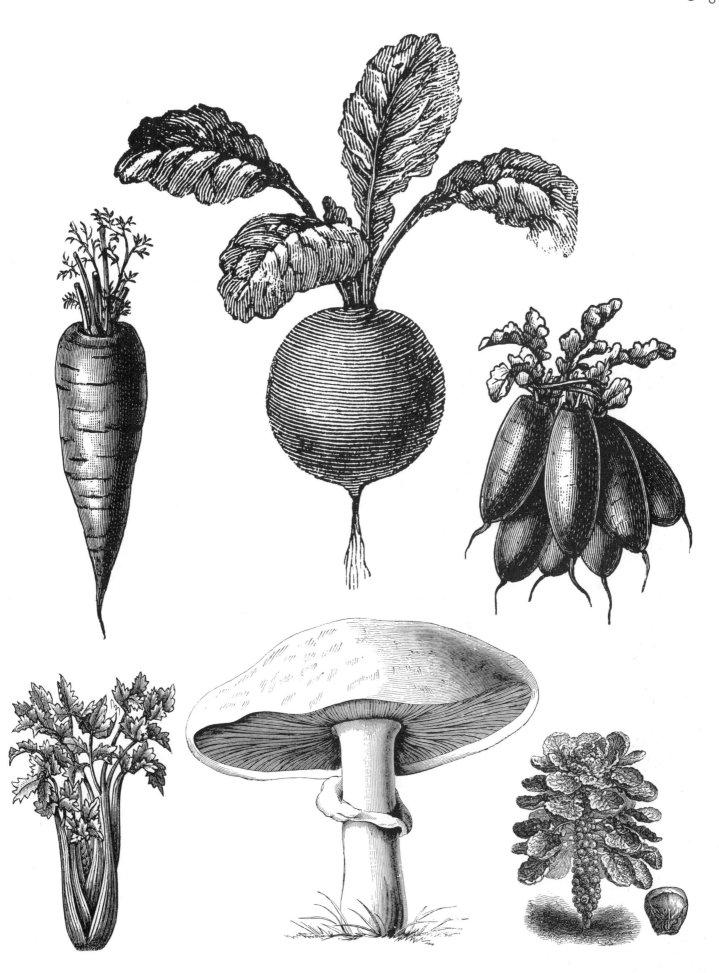

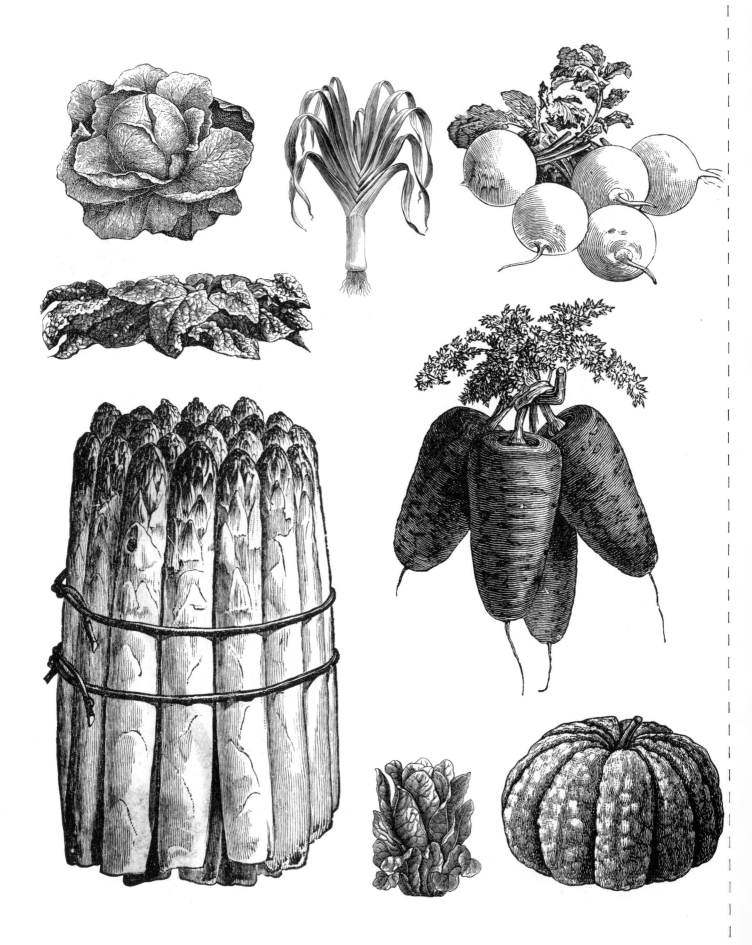

MOTIFS

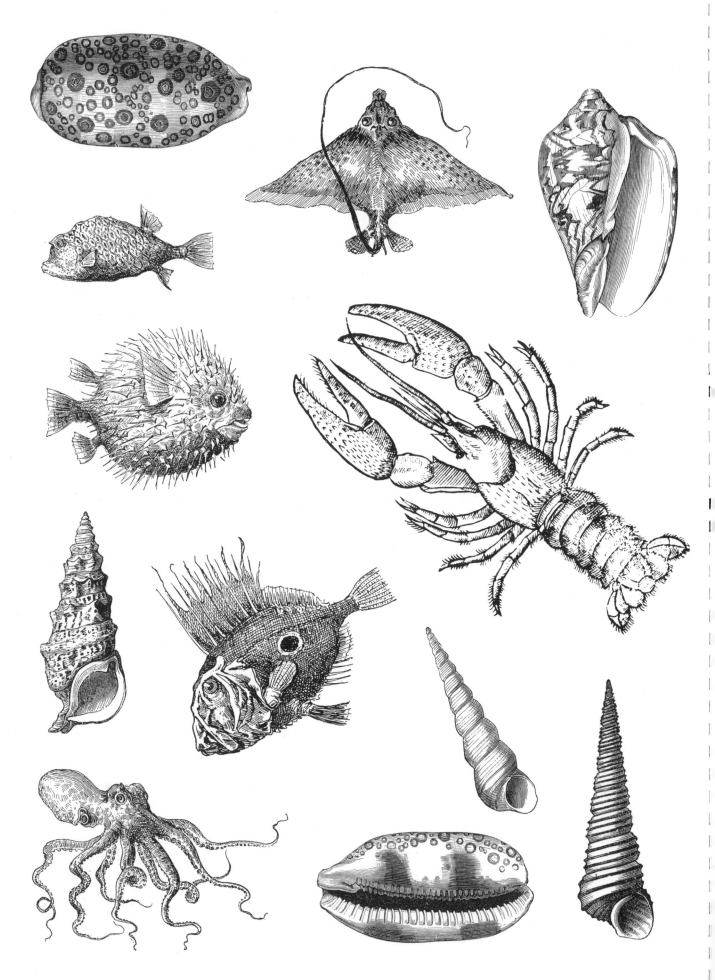

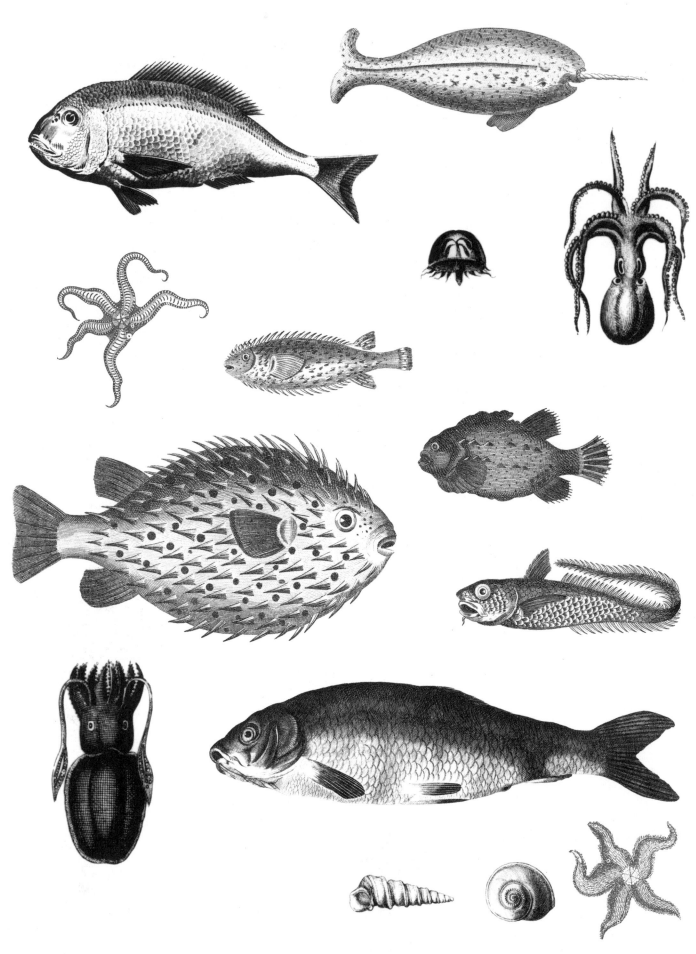

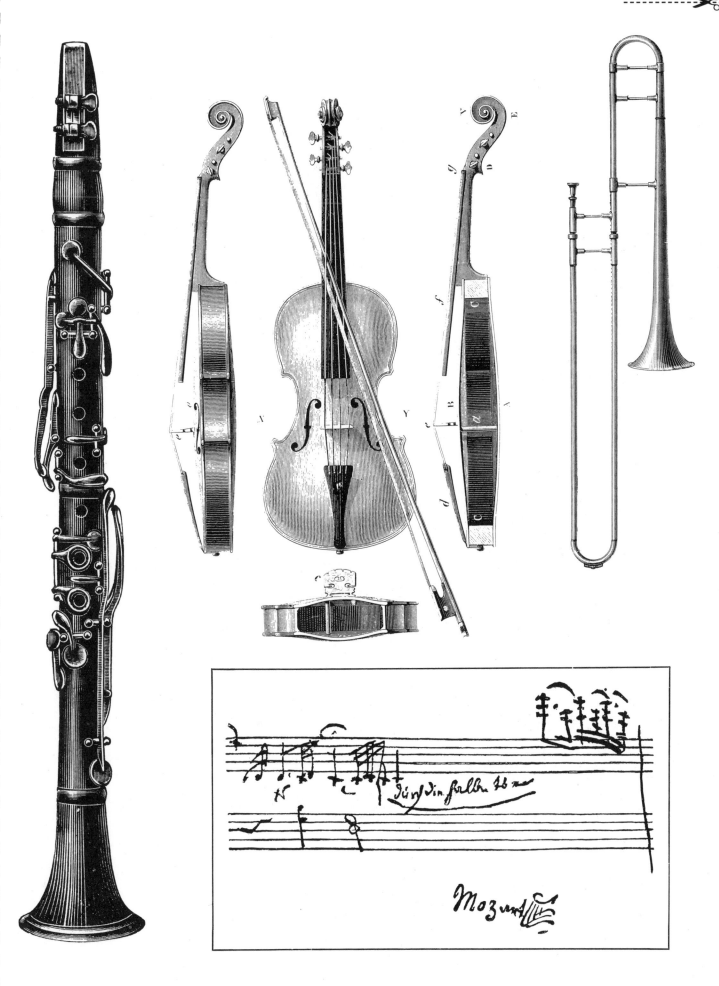

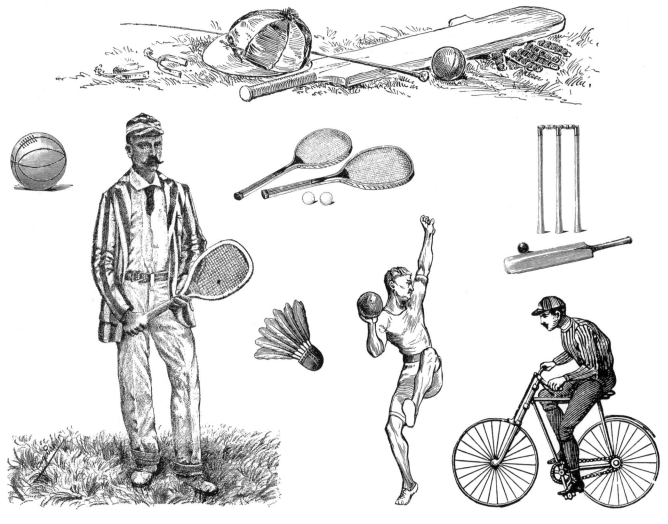

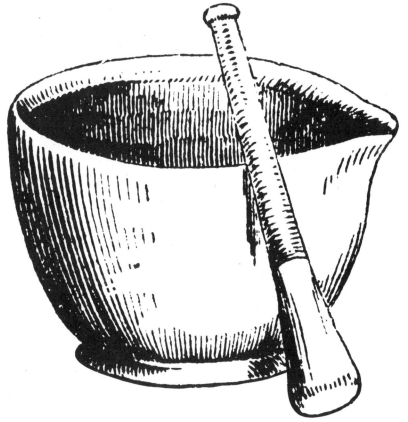

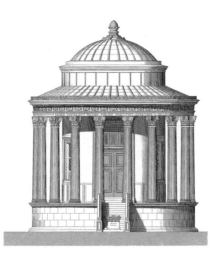

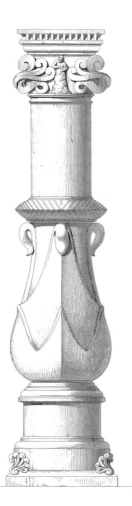

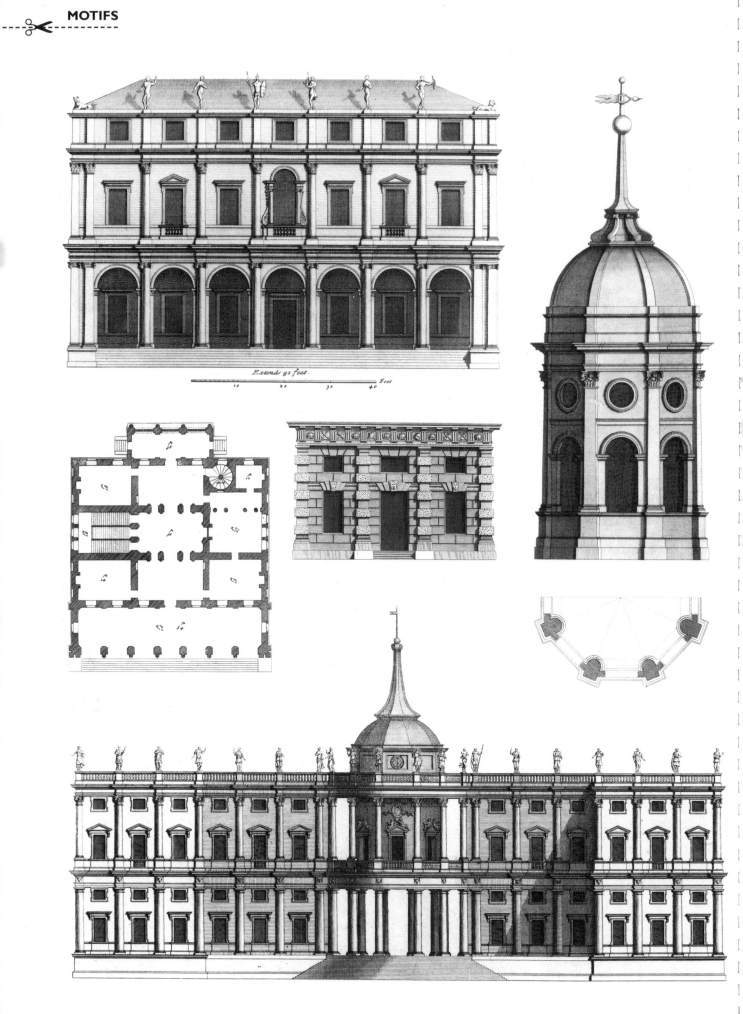

Extends 92 feet.

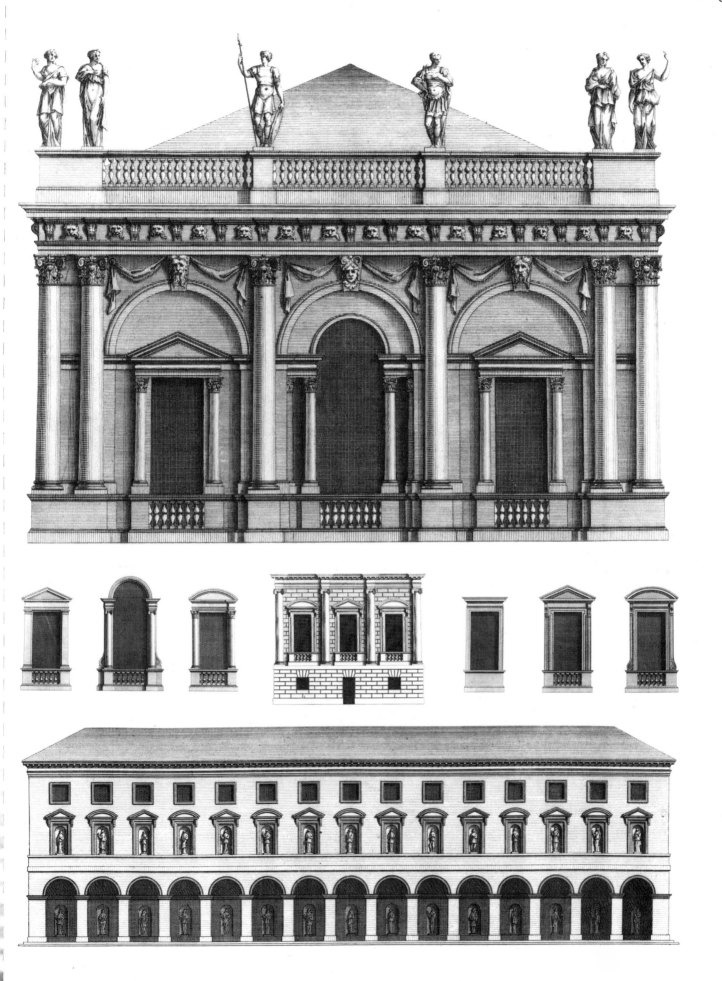

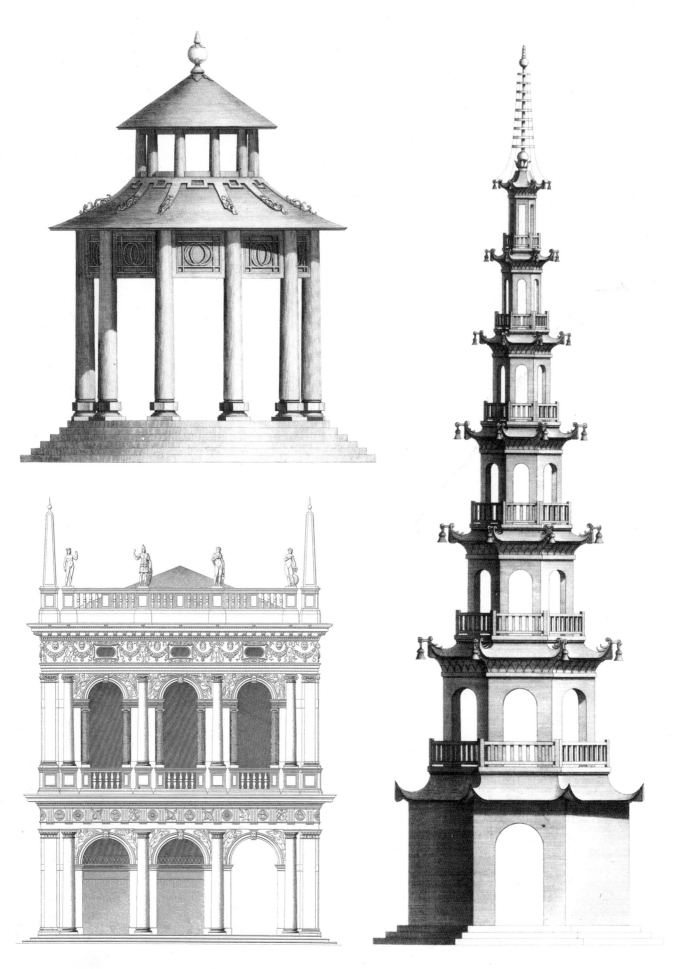

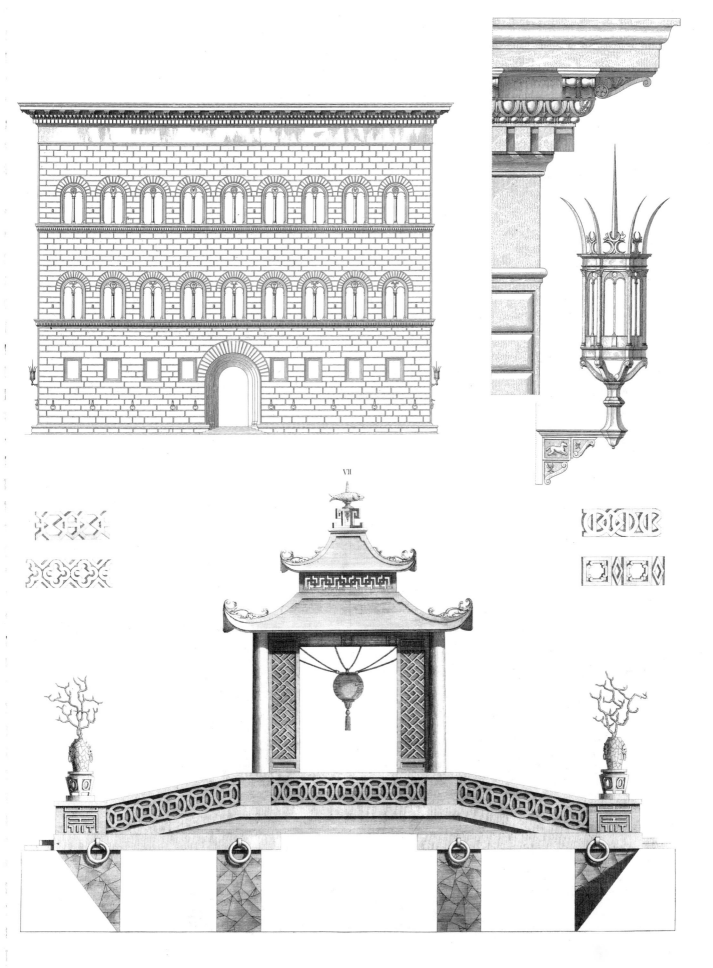

VII

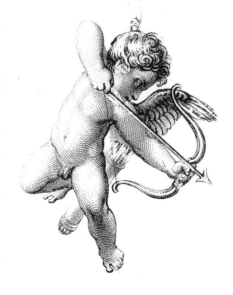

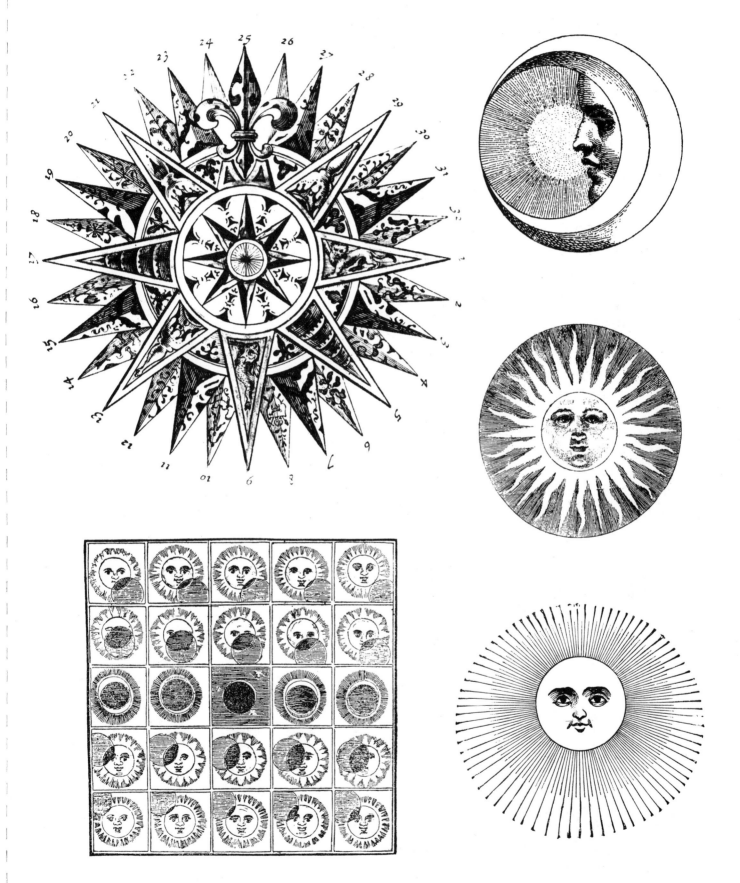

ABCDEFGH
IKLMNOPQ
STUXYZ

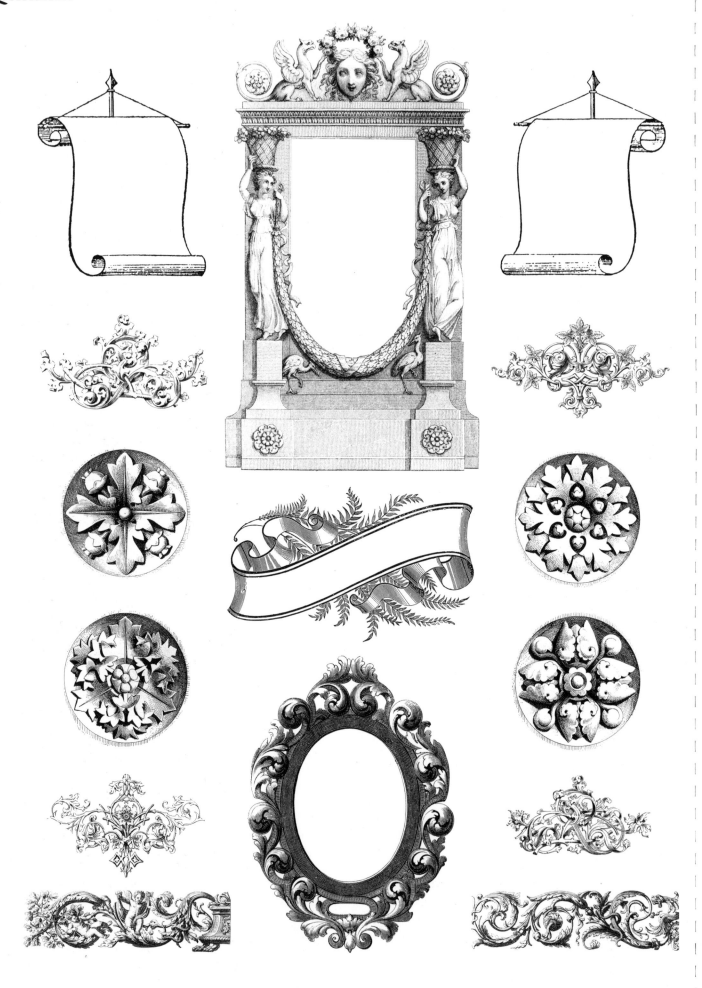

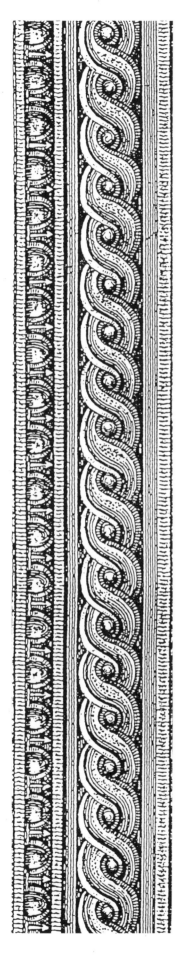

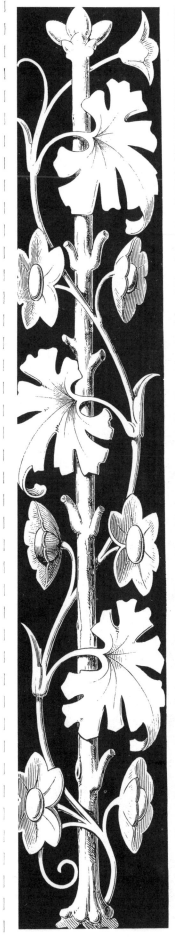

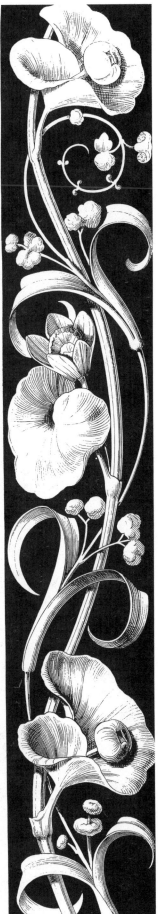

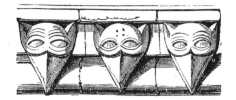

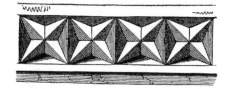

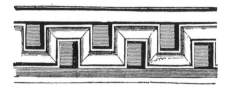